Text © Racheal Cain Stephens, 2019
The moral rights of the author have been asserted.

All rights reserved. No part of this book may be reproduced by any mechanical, photographic or electronic process, or in the form of a phonographic recording; nor may it be stored in a retrieval system, transmitted or otherwise be copied for public or private use, other than for 'fair use' as brief quotations embodied in articles and reviews, without prior written permission of the publisher.

The information given in this book should not be treated as a substitute for professional medical advice; always consult a medical practitioner. Any use of information in this book is at the reader's discretion and risk. Neither the author nor the publisher can be held responsible for any loss, claim or damage arising out of the use, or misuse, of the suggestions made, the failure to take medical advice or for any material on third party websites.

Cover photo and author photo (p.4) by Victoria Cragg

Chapter Art by Safa Amjad

Table of Contents

Foreword 3
The Moment You Realize You Want to Crowdfund 8
Two Months Before Launch 11
One Month Before Launch 20
Final Week Before Launch 31
Launch Day 39
Your Daily Campaign To-Do List 46
Week Two 54
Week Three 57
The Final Week 59
When to Rest 61
Final Thoughts 63

Foreword

Hi there! I'm Racheal and, first of all, I want to congratulate you! If you're reading this, it's already clear: you're a go-getter. You've chosen to not wait any longer for things to just fall into your lap (*they never do, do they?*) but, instead, to go out and make your dreams come true for yourself. So far, rest assured: you're doing everything right. So much of running a successful crowdfunding campaign is in the preparation done beforehand and you're doing just the right thing by digging deep and covering all of your bases now. I applaud you!

Before we dive right in, I wanted to tell you a bit about myself and why I've written this little book. I'm a filmmaker and, in September of 2018, I ran a crowdfunding campaign for my first feature film, ALASKA. In the end, five hundred and twenty-four people came together to help us raise $63,388 toward our production. On top of that, the campaign video got over 66,000 views on Facebook and my Reddit AMA I did for the campaign reached over 44,000 views in just two days! Not only did we raise a big chunk of financing, but we got some really great exposure for the project. It'll all be worth it in the end ... but, alas, it is no easy feat!

I knew, going into it, that $60,000 was going to be a lofty goal so, a few months in advance, I set out to do some serious research. Unfortunately, in all of my digging, I really didn't feel like I was finding ample material or advice to help me in my preparation. My search left me with more questions than answers. *When should I launch? - What should I do to prepare? - Who should I be targeting in my paid ads? - What was the right amount to post daily and what was overkill? - What platforms would have the biggest click-through rates? - What the heck is a click-through rate?!* - There was so much to learn and I was running out of time.

The hard truth is that only 37% of crowdfunding campaigns are successful and, even though ours came out 105% funded in the end, there were still moments in the middle where I wasn't sure if we'd make it all the way. After everything I poured into my campaign for months and months, and witnessing the blood, sweat, and tears other artists were putting into theirs, the very real idea of anyone's campaign being a failure was utterly heartbreaking and horrifying to me.

So that's why I've decided to write this book! I learned *so* much throughout my experience and, though I definitely won't be crowdfunding ever again, I kept thinking how helpful these tips would be to someone just starting out on their journey ... perhaps even helpful enough that they'd save a few projects from making one of the many fatal mistakes which can cause a campaign to fail.

Throughout the pages of this book, I've taken absolutely *everything* I learned while crowdfunding over $60,000 - the things I did right and everything I did very wrong - and I've stripped it all down to basics for you. This book will walk you through your campaign, step-by-step, from the very moment you realize you want to crowdfund one day to your final day of the campaign! My hope is that you'll never feel in the dark like I did and you'll have a stronger sense of whether or not you're on track at every major checkpoint. Deciding to crowdfund requires an enormous, courageous leap of faith and if I can help even just one more creator hit their big goal and make their dream come true, then this will have been worth it to me.

I'd suggest, if you can, to give this entire guide a quick read-through before you jump in, so you have a greater sense of everything that's ahead. From there, feel free to check the boxes as you work your way through each task, highlight important lines, mark it up, and use this book as it was intended: a simple yet complete to-do list to get you from here, point A, all the way until you're finished campaigning!

Before we get started, I should note: while this guide will reference Kickstarter throughout, all of the advice given is applicable to whichever platform you ultimately decide is best for your crowdfunding goals. I went with Kickstarter simply because it had the highest organic traffic and because I had friends who had run successful Kickstarter campaigns (including friends who had paid for the expensive $5,000+ Kickstarter coaches) who helped me tremendously. (All of that advice is baked into this book: *lucky you!*) In the end, I was very happy with my choice to use Kickstarter, but this guide will translate across the board for any platform (Indiegogo, GoFundMe, Seed&Spark etc.).

Also, I launched my campaign to raise financing for a feature film. The examples given in this book will be geared toward creative projects, but I know they'll be beneficial for any campaign and for raising any goal amount under $60,000! Even if you're just looking to raise $20,000, these tips should get you there (*and, if followed, I bet will get you much more than you asked for)!*

Lastly, I feel I must warn you: what you're about to embark on will change you to your core and challenge you in ways most couldn't ever dream of. You're about to get your hands dirty, get raw and vulnerable, and be forced to go bigger than you've ever gone before. But you know you can do it because you wouldn't be reading this otherwise. There's a lot to learn and it's going to be hard, hard work but the thing I hope you take away from this little book most of all is that it's absolutely 100% possible for you to hit those big goals. It is more than possible.

Excited yet? Nervous? Good! Now let's raise that money to make your dreams come true.

The Moment You Realize You Want to Crowdfund

It'll hit you right in your gut. A deep sense of resolve with a sucker punch of excitement and an explosion of a million nervous butterflies. The decision to run a crowdfunding campaign is a big one and shouldn't be made lightly. The work that goes into these things can be gargantuan and, these days, it seems you've only got one chance to get your campaign right. The moment you decide you want to crowdfund one day is a big one and once it hits, that big countdown-until-launch-day starts ticking away.

I'd say running a successful Kickstarter is 85% in your preparation. The more time you can give to the tasks in this section, to grow an audience and cover all of your bases, the better - but, ideally, you're starting at least roughly three months out from when you intend to launch your campaign. Maybe you need to go live in exactly three months or perhaps you've got no rush; doesn't matter. Whenever the moment strikes and you know for certain you'll be crowdfunding one day, I would immediately do these few following things:

☐ START BUILDING YOUR AUDIENCE

Set up an email capture on any websites you run. If you run any sites (personal or for the project) immediately set up an email capture pop-up box to start collecting emails from your site visitors. You can use Mailchimp to do this. Build a solid email list that you can hit up on day one and at major milestones throughout your campaign.

Create a Facebook page for your project, as early on as possible. You can create an Instagram and Twitter for your project too, but definitely steer your efforts toward building out your project's Facebook Page. Facebook is going to be your biggest ally.

Build out your personal Facebook network as much as you can. Now is the time to accept all of those lingering friend requests and add all of those "People You May Know" Facebook has been suggesting you add. The bigger your network becomes now, the better.

☐ GET OUT AND BE SOCIAL

Attend those mixers your friends keep inviting you to. Show up to the parties you may have turned down before. And while you're at these events, start talking about the campaign with those you meet! Even if your launch date is still a few months out, start getting it on peoples' radars now. Ask anyone who has run a crowdfunding campaign for their biggest tips (trust me, they love to share what they learned) and make people feel a part of the project. These campaigns are all about coming out of your shell and making people feel included in what you're passionate about, so get out and get started now!

Two Months Before Launch

Note: When I was preparing for my campaign, I was bartending part-time in the evenings and treated my campaign prep as my full time gig. If you already have a full time job, separate from your project, you may want to spread out the work in this next section more thinly, starting three months out from your ideal launch date rather than two.

☐ BUILD OUT YOUR CORE TEAM

Avoid a common fatal error and build yourself a solid, talented team just for crowdfunding. This will be one of the most crucial steps in determining whether or not your campaign will be successful. Clearly you're an independent do-it-yourselfer but, trust me, you are not going to be able to go this one alone. I repeat: You ARE NOT going to be able to do this alone! One of my biggest mistakes was thinking that if I worked hard enough and fast enough, I wouldn't have to rely on others as much throughout the process. Looking back, I could've gone much further and gotten so much more out of the experience had I done the work in the two months beforehand of building out a proper core team for support. It's estimated that each member of your team should be able to pull in roughly $5k on their own. So if you're looking to raise $50,000, you're going to need to bring on 9 other people to help you hit your goal.

Be strategic here. **Try to bring on people who are naturally active and vocal on social media, especially Facebook.** Ideally, these people have a big presence and following of their own.

Aim to bring on team members with entirely separate networks from your own. Your mother or childhood friend would probably work their butts off for your campaign but, keep in mind, there's going to be a lot of overlap in your social networks there, meaning the same people are going to see the campaign over and over again. Try to bring on team members who may be in a similar field as you, but have entirely different networks.

As incentive, if you're working on a creative project, like a film or music album, you can approach people you think would naturally make great crowdfunding team members and offer them an "Associate Producer" or "Production Associate" credit on your project (or something similar) to get them excited about it.

The beautiful thing about crowdfunding a film was that I naturally already had a team for the project (cast, crew, producers) who could help me share it. Even if they can't commit to being a core team member, who will help with the daily actions required, get your project's entire team and your main network of friends involved early on so they know the campaign is coming and are prepared to help!

☐ SET YOUR GOAL AMOUNT

Once you know how many key players you have on your core crowdfunding team, you can go ahead and set your goal amount.

Do you have 9 strong team members, aside from yourself, you're confident can bring in $5k on their own? - Then go ahead and set your goal to $60,000. Could you only find 8? - Consider knocking it down to $55,000. (And so on.)

Choosing your goal amount is a CRUCIAL decision, especially if you choose to use Kickstarter as your platform, as it's all-or-nothing (you must hit your entire goal or get nothing). You absolutely have to set a realistic goal. How does the number make you feel? - *Your goal amount shouldn't give you anxiety.* You should feel confident and optimistic you'll be able to hit it and even go over. I'd have to guess the pretty low success rate of Kickstarter campaigns is due to unrealistic expectations. Remember: you can always go over, but you can't come up short!

They say the majority of successful campaigns hit 30% funded within their first 48 hours. Days one and two are absolutely crucial days in setting the tone and determining the success of your campaign. It feels really icky and weird to look at people you love in terms of how much they might give to your campaign, but you should definitely be realistic about where your own personal network can get you. The majority of the money you raise in your first 48 hours, before it has had the chance to organically spread and get any internal Kickstarter promotion, is going to be your "love money", or money from your own family and friends. Be mindful that this "love money" should ideally get you to at least 30% of your goal amount.

☐ CHOOSE A STRATEGIC LAUNCH DATE

Again, the first few days of your campaign are going to be your biggest days, by far! They're going to be absolutely pivotal in setting the tone for the entirety of your campaign. For this reason, be really strategic about the dates you choose to launch on.

In terms of which months of the year, the sweet spot for crowdfunding is said to be from February to late May. The idea is, the later in the year you get, the harder it is to launch because people are out spending for the holidays and don't have the extra cash to fork out for your campaign. However, oftentimes you may not have the choice for which time of the year to launch and you'll need to launch whenever works best for you and your project's timeline. Don't sweat it too much!

Just make sure to launch on a Tuesday or a Wednesday. By doing this, both your first 48-hour window and your campaign's final days will all fall mid-week. Making sure these crucial days of your campaign fall on strong days for social media activity is imperative and Tuesdays, Wednesdays and Thursdays are, by far, when people are most active online!

Finally, learn from one of my biggest mistakes and do not launch your campaign before a holiday weekend! In the craziness of planning for my campaign, I totally missed this and we went pretty silent on the first weekend of my campaign because everyone was out BBQing and swimming to celebrate Labor Day weekend. Ultimately, our first weekend ended up being much slower than I would have liked, which forced me to hustle even more in the weeks to come. Learn from my mistake and consider all major national holidays when you're choosing when to launch!

☐ CREATE A KILLER CAMPAIGN VIDEO

Shoot your video for your campaign at least two months out so that you're not scrambling to edit it near your launch date. Call in favors, borrow equipment from friends, select a cool location (bonus points if the setting has anything to do with the project), and shoot a high quality campaign video that will hook viewers and make them want to be a part of your vision.

Make it personal. Most of the time, Kickstarter backers are investing in you. Show off your personality, your passion, and build trust in the vision. Storytelling is so important here. *What led you to start this project in the first place? What keeps you motivated?* Especially when it comes to campaigns for creative projects, people need to know your story to want to be a part of that story. I had two complete strangers give me $1,000 each and one of them reached out to tell me he was giving me the money simply because he was impressed by how long I had been working on it and wanted to support my "tenacity". Make sure you keep your video personal.

Keep it short. I was surprised to find that most people didn't even finish my three and a half minute campaign video and were dropping out after about two minutes. Put the bulk of your most important information and most catchy visuals up front, within the first minute of your video. We all know attention spans are at an all-time low. You want to keep peoples' interest so they're not clicking away before any great content. Keep it tight and concise!

Highlight your rewards. Make sure you talk a bit about your perks and what backers will be receiving in the end. People want to know what's in it for them!

Include a call to action. Literally say out loud what you want the viewers of your campaign video to do. For example: "Please contribute what you can, follow the campaign, and share it with your friends and family" works. I said this out loud throughout my video and then even had a call-to-action title card at the end of the video reiterating exactly how to help.

Use B-roll and cutaways of you, your team, and your product in action. It's important to make it clear that your project is already underway and thoroughly developed to help build your audience's confidence in you as a creator. Kickstarter backers are essentially investors in your vision and you want to attract them by showing as much of your product or project in action as possible.

☐ DECIDE ON ANY CAMPAIGN EVENTS YOU'LL RUN

To keep your crowdfunding campaign exciting throughout the month it's live, I highly recommend planning a different big event for each different week of your campaign. For example, for during my second week, I had previously lined up a matching donor who agreed to match any pledges made to our campaign within a 72-hour period and then I promoted the heck out of that event. In week three, I held a different sweepstakes, Monday-Friday, where new backers were entered into a small daily raffle to win prizes such as an invite to the film's wrap party, high quality photos of their name on a film slate, or limited edition movie t-shirts. I also rolled out new perks, such as actual props from my film to motivate people to jump and pledge immediately. And in week four, I ran a big "Face Your Fears Challenge" where one pledge (or any upped pledge) counted as one vote toward which big fear I was going to have to face that October. (Bonus Tip: People LOVE to make you do things.)

The more creative you can get with these, the more people will take notice and remain engaged. (It'll also give you so much more to post about when you're trying to hit your 5-7 daily post marks later too!) There is so much you can do for these events but, most importantly, just keep them fun! By the end, even I was getting bored with sharing the same information, day after day, so imagine how your audience feels. Keep it fresh.

It's important to line these events up now, as you'll have to prepare for them by getting any matching donors to commit, creating graphics for the events, ordering sweepstakes prizes, etc.

☐ CREATE A SHAREABLE CALENDER FOR YOUR CAMPAIGN

By the end of your first month of prep, with a month left to go, you should ideally have a bird's eye view of your overall timeline for your campaign. This includes the date of launch, the halfway point, your final 72, 48, and 24 hours, and each week's different big event with their start dates and end dates.

Create a shareable calendar with all of this information and share it with your core team to get everyone on the same page regarding the timeline. One month to go! Get them hyped for your impending launch!

One Month Before Launch

Four weeks left 'til launch day. You got this!

☐ START BUILDING OUT YOUR CAMPAIGN PAGE

With four weeks left to go before launch, if you haven't yet, now is the time to get into Kickstarter (or whichever platform you've chosen) and start building out your campaign page! Give yourself time to familiarize yourself with the way the website works and how to navigate around it. The quicker you can move around and make necessary changes, the more efficient you'll be when it counts later. Building out my campaign page took me longer than expected and it's so crucial to get this right, since this page will be the face of your campaign and the landing page for all of your hard work.

You should aim to have your entire campaign page filled out and looking perfect with at least a full week left before your launch date. As soon as you think it's ready, you're going to have to get your campaign approved by Kickstarter and, while it only ended up taking them a few hours to approve mine, if they encounter any issues, sometimes that process can take up to a few days.

CREATE YOUR MASTER "PAD" LIST

Build out a "PAD" list for yourself. PAD stands for Personal, Acquaintance, and Do Not Contact. Facebook will allow you to export a list of all of your Facebook friends, including the phone numbers and emails of everyone who has included that info in their profile. (Side note: also add any of those friends' emails to your original email list you've been building through Mailchimp!) This list will come in handy SO much and keep you organized throughout the campaign.

Take the initial list and move it into Microsoft Excel where you can reorder it and organize it into these three sections. First: **Personal.** These are all of your personal contacts or friends, who will be the most likely to donate to your campaign. Next, **Acquaintance.** In this section, I grouped all of the people I hadn't spoken to in awhile and Facebook friends I quite honestly didn't know where they had come from. (If you were accepting all of those outstanding friend requests like I mentioned earlier, this is probably where those people will go.) Finally, **Do Not Contact**. This section should lie at the bottom of your list and include anyone you would shudder to think of reaching out to. Campaigning can be awkward enough, let's not make it even more complicated!

From there, I went even further and organized my Personal and Acquaintance sections by how I knew them. I grouped them into sections like "Family" "Elementary School" "High School" "College" "Work" and "Social Media Acquaintances". Going through each list was like revisiting different eras of my life. Believe it or not, this will actually come in handy so much later on, when you're crafting and personalizing your initial ask messages!

Finally, after I had them grouped, I ordered them in order of who I thought would be most likely to donate. This seems like a lot of work but, when you're working with a finite amount of time, it's important to be super intentional about where you spend it. Building this "PAD" list is one of the most important steps of preparation so don't rush it. It will pay off!

☐ CHOOSE YOUR REWARD LEVELS & PERKS

As part of building out your campaign page this month, it's time to decide on which perks to offer your backers. You will know better than anyone what your community wants. Think of the things that would get you excited to back a project. Offer copies of your work in different formats and fun, unique experiences only you can provide.

Be strategic about your reward levels. My lowest perk level was $5 and my highest was $5,000. I had a $25 perk where backers could receive a digital download of the film the day after our world premiere, but for only $5 more they could have their names included in the credits of the film. That translated to people who would've likely donated just $25 bumping their pledge up a couple bucks and giving $30 to have their name in the credits. For my campaign, there were a few reward levels that were clearly most popular amongst my backers. Here's the actual screengrab of my reward level popularity:

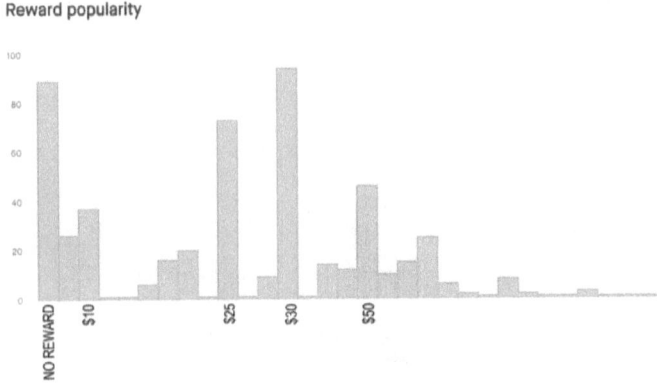

You can see that, aside from "No Reward", my most popular levels were $10, $25, $30 and $50. Be sure to include these levels.

Offer mostly e-perks, or perks which can be delivered online. When considering what to offer backers as their perks, set yourself up for success and create rewards like digital downloads of artwork, MP3s of your soundtrack, or high quality images that can be emailed. Limit the number of actual physical perks you'll be required to ship out to people because, not only will this be a time consuming headache to keep organized, but those shipping costs will eat away at your pledge money in the end.

Include a social media shout-out perk option. This was my $10 reward level. For every $10 pledge, I would add the backer on Facebook (if we weren't already "friends") and then make a post to their Facebook wall with a personalized, eye-catching GIF, thanking them for their pledge. I started every single shout-out post with something like: "Hey ___! Thank you so much for contributing to alaskakickstarter.com! We're so excited to have your support" ... (and so on). Here's an example of one of these shout-outs:

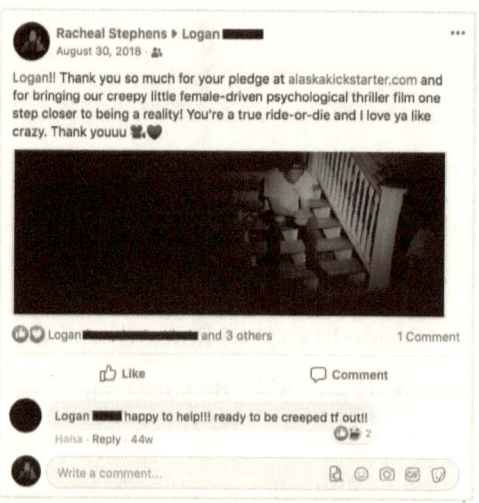

The key here is to both tag the person's name and include the campaign URL in the very first line of the post. This way, you're cross-promoting and activating that backer's entire Facebook network while instantly fulfilling your perk. Anyone who sees your flashy GIF post to their friend's wall will immediately see the link to the campaign at the top. This perk became a super successful promotional tool for us, while also being a fun way to make our backers feel seen, included, and proud to support us!

Offer some limited-edition perks. Rest assured, you'll be able to add, delete, or adjust the available quantity of your perks at any moment throughout your campaign. I found limited-edition perks to be really helpful in the middle zone (weeks two and three) in getting people to take action and pledge instantly, before the perks were gone. I offered things like limited-edition t-shirts and actual props from my film, and then would announce them as soon as they were available. I had several of these limited-edition items claimed within just minutes of posting them! I also heard from several friends that having these perks sprinkled throughout the course of the campaign kept it (and my constant updates about it) more exciting too.

Finally, be sure to offer a few in-person, hands-on experiences. These tend to be very successful perks for your higher-level backers. Get creative and think of things that only you will be able to offer. For my campaign, I offered walk-on roles in my film and on-set behind-the-scenes experiences for people with a little more money to throw down.

Note: If you're going to offer any in-person experiences, though, make sure to state in your perk description that "travel and lodging is not included" with their pledge and they "must be available for the experience when it occurs".

(Here's an example of one of these perk descriptions:)

> Pledge $750 or more
>
> BE AN EXTRA IN A LOS ANGELES SCENE!
>
> With this limited perk, you'll be invited to set to be an extra in a big scene filmed in Los Angeles!
> *Transportation and housing not included. Must be available for the shoot days*

☐ PREP ALL OF YOUR VISUAL CONTENT

With at least a month left to go before launch, you should start prepping all of your visual content for your campaign. This means any and all photos, graphics, ads, etc. you're going to be sharing.

My team and I changed our cover photos on Facebook every day of the campaign, with the number of days left featured in the top corner.

Here's an example of one of those cover photos:

I made sure I had all of those cover images prepared in advance, so that I could easily share them in my morning email to our core team and didn't have to worry about photoshopping any of these together on the day of. I also had banners and graphics made for every event I was going to run.

Note: If you aren't experienced with graphic design or don't want to spend a lot of your own time here, consider outsourcing some of the design work to an artist on Fiverr.com. You can have beautiful graphics made quickly by any of their hundreds of artists for as little as $5!

Another way I prepped content was I did a photoshoot with a photographer friend in LA, about a month before my campaign launched. That gave me a pool of over fifty high-quality images of myself for posting throughout the campaign.

Here are a few examples of what those photos looked like:

I thanked myself *so* many times during the campaign for spending the time to have those photos taken beforehand! The truth is, people want to see people and photos of you are always going to perform best. Have a few great photos of yourself prepared so that you can be changing your profile picture frequently and harnessing the power of those Facebook algorithms during your campaign!

Nothing is more guaranteed to land on a friend's newsfeed than your newly-changed profile picture but, during your campaign, you're barely going to have time to brush your hair in the morning, let alone take nice photos of yourself. Prepare ahead of time! Now's the time to get those headshots redone. Hire a professional and get some cool artist photos taken.

Remember, this is a CAMPAIGN and these photos will become your visual arsenal. The more creative and "on-brand", the better.

☐ HOST A CORE TEAM MEETING

Now that you've got your core team assembled, it's important to keep them looped in on the progress and everything they're going to be responsible for next month. Host a core team meeting with any local team members to build team moral and get some valuable face-time before you're in the trenches together for the next few weeks. Throw a pizza party or host team drinks! Remember, each team member is going to be pulling in $5,000 for you over the next month, so it's important to make them feel appreciated.

Have them build their own "PAD" lists, add them as "administrators" to the project Facebook page, and go through exactly what their daily campaign tasks will be (Page 48) so that they can be prepared for the upcoming workload.

☐ BONUS TIP: GET PRESS TO COVER YOUR CAMPAIGN

I'm including this as a bonus tip because I wanted to do this for myself but ran out of time and didn't get to. Bummer dude. But if you find you do have the time, go ahead and try to get a few press outlets to do write-ups of your campaign! You can do this by writing up a one page "press release" about the project, including any major press hooks for your project, and then sending it to any online outlets you think might be interested. Cross-reference and do your research to find if any press has covered similar campaigns in the past.

It's important to do this around four weeks out from launch so that any press you get will come out right before you launch or during the first week or two of your campaign. Press will help legitimize your project and build confidence in backers, and outlets are constantly looking for fresh material to cover!

Final Week Before Launch

Crunch time, baby. Welcome to the home stretch!

☐ DECIDE ON A CUSTOM URL FOR YOUR PROJECT

The moment you launch next week, Kickstarter (or whichever platform you choose) is going to automatically generate a random URL for your project. It'll be a long link with a bunch of random letters and numbers.

Instead of using this, we're going to create a custom, clean and concise URL for your project. I'll go through exactly how to do this in the next section but, for now, just decide on what your campaign URL will be. Mine was ALASKAKICKSTARTER.COM.

Come up with something creative and clear that will look clean and simple in all of the posts you'll make next month. It should be easy to remember, so people will have an easier time sharing your campaign link via word of mouth. Once you have it picked, run a search at GoDaddy.com to make sure the domain is available.

☐ SCHEDULE ALL OF YOUR CAMPAIGN EMAILS

Remember that email list I told you to start building earlier? Now's the time to start using it!

If you use Gmail, go ahead and download the add-on called Boomerang. It's an extremely helpful tool that acts as a plug-in to your normal account which will allow you to schedule out emails to be sent automatically at any designated day and time in the future! In your week before launch, use Boomerang to schedule out 30 emails to people on your email list to be sent our per day.

I used the headline **"ALASKA Feature Film is LIVE on Kickstarter!"** in every email. You can create something similar for yours. From there, write 1-2 custom, personalized sentences addressing the person you're emailing. Then, use a blurb that can be copy and pasted into the body of each email so that you can work through these emails quickly. **Just make sure to always include the custom URL you just came up with.**

Here's an example of what this email could look like:

Hi ____!

[1-2 CUSTOM PERSONALIZED SENTENCES ADDRESSING THE SPECIFIC PERSON.] I wanted to reach out personally to tell you about an exciting project I'm working on and ask for your help.

We've launched a [PROJECT TYPE] called [TITLE]. [ONE SENTENCE ON WHAT IT'S ABOUT.] [ONE SENTENCE ABOUT WHY YOU'RE PASSIONATE ABOUT IT (I'm passionate about it because...)]

So I am totally gonna ask you for two personal favors: can you go to our fundraising site and donate? And, more importantly, can you post our campaign on your Facebook and Twitter pages? It would really mean a lot to me.

To donate go to www.CUSTOMURL.com, choose your perk level at the amount you're willing to give, and then use the share button there on the site to post it to your Facebook and Twitter pages. [SUGGEST A PERK: I thought you might particularly like the early-bird DVD special.]

Thank you for allowing me the chance to reach out to you directly. This [PROJECT TYPE] means the world to me and I can't thank you enough for any support you're willing to give. Thank you, FIRSTNAME!

Sincerely,
YOUR NAME
www.CUSTOMURL.COM

Feel free to use this exact email or spruce it up to sound more like you! The more personal and inclusive you can make it sound, the more effective it'll be.

Just make sure you schedule out an email to every person on your email list you've been compiling via Mailchimp (and your exported Facebook friends' list), hitting the maximum amount Boomerang will allow you to schedule per each day. This will free up so much valuable time next week for doing what counts!

☐ SCHEDULE OUT YOUR SOCIAL MEDIA POSTS

When we get into your campaign daily to-do list, you're going to have a large target of making 5-7 Facebook posts, sending 5-7 Tweets, and posting 1 Instagram post per day. I know - *it sounds like a lot* - and it is! To help cut down on this huge task, harness the power of scheduling out some of these posts in this week ahead of time. For $15, I registered for **Hootsuite** for just the month of the campaign and scheduled out all of my tweets so that I never had to touch my Twitter account unless I had something specific or important to say.

I wanted to be a bit more organic with the Instagram and Facebook posts, so I scheduled only a few Instagram posts to go out at key moments in the campaign, such as our launch day, our halfway point, and our final 72, 48, and 24 hours. For the Facebook, I scheduled posts for these key moments as well, along with posts about all of our perks that I knew would remain the same throughout the campaign.

There's so much you can say in advance! The more you can schedule now, the more you'll thank yourself later when you're working to hit those daily targets. You'll feel like you have ten clones of yourself working to post your social media and it'll feel amazing.

Absolutely make sure that you're always including your custom URL in every post that you make and that you're including it in the very first line. Any posts that you make to Facebook and Instagram, longer than a few lines, will get chopped off so make sure that your URL is at the very top so it's the first thing people will see. It's all about making it as easy as possible for people to find your URL and get to your campaign page to donate!

☐ CREATE A FACEBOOK EVENT FOR LAUNCH DAY

Three days before launch, create a Facebook event for your campaign's big launch day and invite the maximum that Facebook will allow you which is 500 people. Set the date to your launch day and set the time to 1pm so that people will be alerted during their weekday lunchtime, after the campaign has had a few hours to accrue some healthy pledges. Invite some of your core team members to be co-hosts alongside you, so that they can invite some of their "Personal" contacts from their PAD list. We'll create more of these events later, throughout key moments of your campaign but it's important that the 500 people you invite to this first event are high up on your lists as "highly likely to donate". Here's what my event looked like:

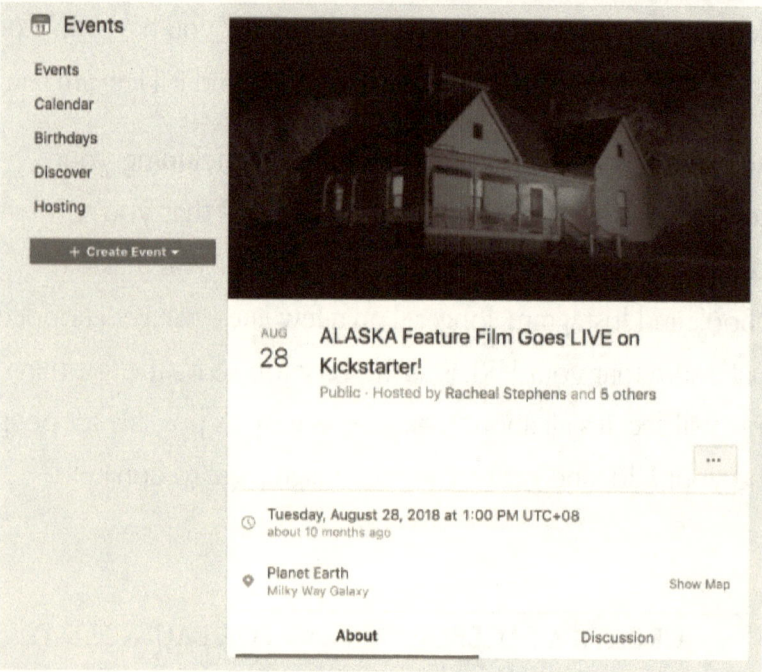

This is such an easy way to instantly activate 500 people from your friend's list to let them know about your campaign. From there, whether they respond to your event invite or not, Facebook will automatically remind them when the event is coming up and also alert them when it's gone live.

☐ JOIN FACEBOOK PAGES WITH SIMILAR AUDIENCES

Request to be in as many Facebook groups with similar audiences as you can find. I was crowdfunding a horror film, so I joined every "Horror Movie Lover"/ "Halloween Junkie" Facebook group I could think of. Think about what groups your target audience would be in.

You'll be posting in these groups during the campaign but you'll want to request to join them with at least 3 days before launch, because any private groups can take up to a few days to approve you and welcome you to the group.

☐ LINE UP 3-5 EARLY DONORS

Line up 3-5 early donors who will donate the moment your campaign launches so that no one else ever sees the amount at $0.00 or the backer count at zero. I had my mom, my brother, and my best friend, who I knew were going to donate, do this and, within minutes, the campaign had raised over $400. (Very generous of them, I know.)

BONUS TIP: MAKE YOUR INSTAGRAM A BUSINESS PAGE

If you can, make your Instagram a Business page so that you can utilize the "swipe-up" feature in your Instagram's "Stories" which will send people directly to the campaign site. Essentially, you just want to do the work for people and make it as easy as possible for them to find your page and contribute.

You can do this by going to "Edit Profile" on your Instagram profile and then clicking "Get More Tools". This will take you to where you can change it.

Launch Day

You made it!!! CONGRATULATIONS!

Now throw all of your shame and inhibitions out the window because it's time to go bigger than you've ever gone before!

☐ **CREATE YOUR CUSTOM URL FOR YOUR PROJECT**

The moment you launch, take the random URL Kickstarter has generated for you and replace it with the short and clear custom URL you came up with last week.

First, purchase your custom domain for the month through GoDaddy.com.

Then, set up a basic redirect so that people visiting the primary domain will be redirected to the subdomain. (Your custom URL (ALASKAKICKSTARTER.COM, etc.) will be your "primary domain" and the random URL Kickstarter created will be the "subdomain".) In the GoDaddy 'Domain Settings' tab, look for 'Forwarding' > 'Domain' and click on 'Manage'.

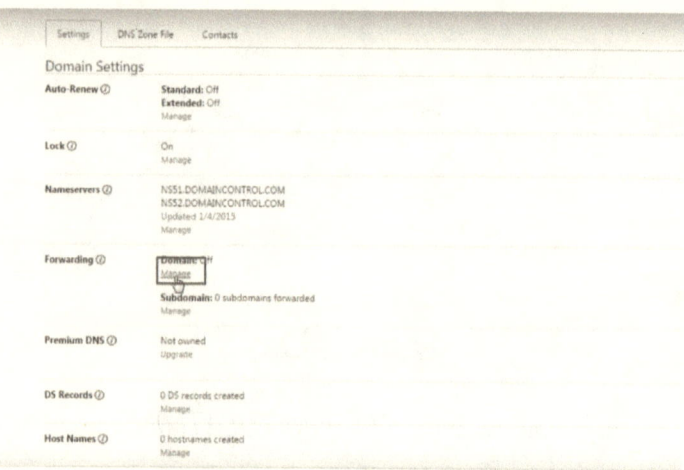

From the popup window select 'Add Forwarding'.

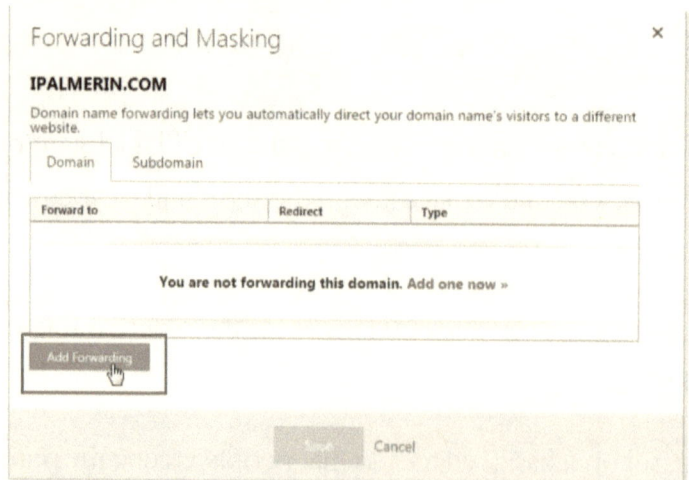

Leave the 'Forward to' field as 'https://' and type in the subdomain (www.yourdomain.com). Leave the other settings as they are. Click 'Add', then click 'Save'.

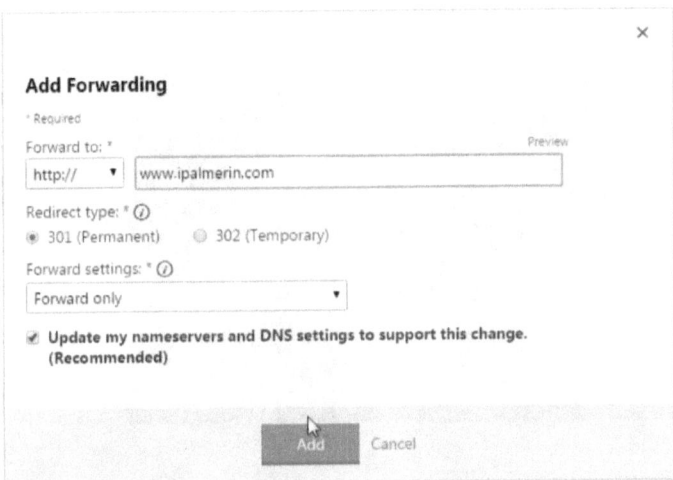

In just a few moments your primary domain should redirect automatically to your subdomain. Your custom URL is live!

☐ UPLOAD YOUR CAMPAIGN VIDEO TO YOUR FACEBOOK PAGE

Immediately after launch, upload your campaign video to your project's Facebook page and pin it to the top of your page, that way it's the very first thing anyone sees when they visit your page. Include your new custom URL in the video title.

Here's what my pinned video post looked like:

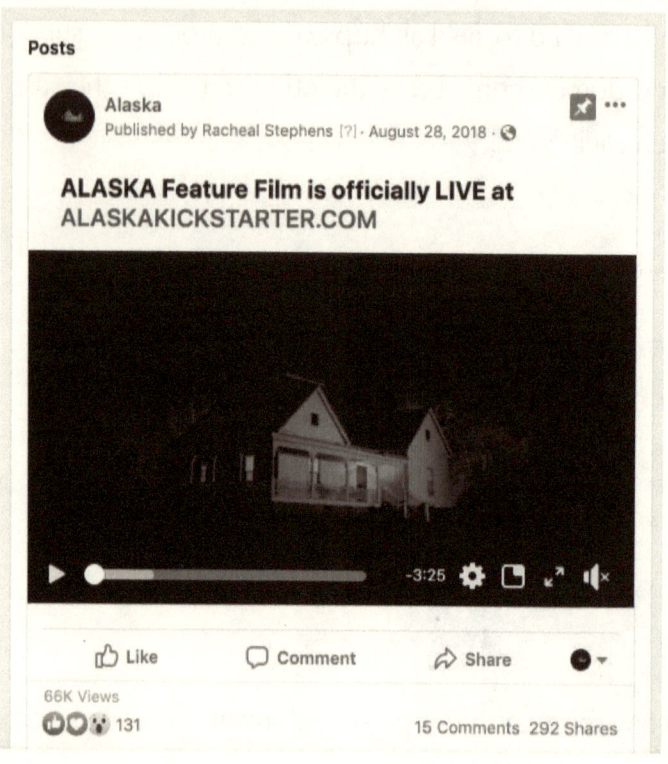

☐ PROMOTE YOUR CAMPAIGN VIDEO WITH TARGETED ADS

You know how they say 'It takes money to make money'? ... If you can afford to right now, run some targeted ads for your campaign video. This will help generate buzz and, by making the URL easily accessible, will send traffic to your campaign page.

Under "Boost Post", define your audience, budget and schedule.

Your "Lifetime Budget" is where you'll set how much you want to spend, in total, on these ads. I decided on $100 for the entire month. (Considering we garnered over 66,000 views in just those 30 days, I felt it was worth it and ultimately earned us much more than we spent.)

In "Schedule", set your ad promotion to end as soon as your campaign will come to a close.

For your "Audience", the targeting is extremely important. You want to activate your friends and family's networks and then work out from there. Boost your post using these audience parameters:

-**People who like your page and their friends**

-**Ages 18-65+**

-**Living in United States and United Kingdom**

☐ SEND YOUR FIRST MORNING EMAIL TO YOUR CORE TEAM

It's time to send your first morning team email! This first launch day email is important! Congratulate your core team on all of their hard work and dedication to get to this point and use fun GIFs to spice it up and make it sound more like you.

What sets your launch day morning team email apart from the other morning emails you'll be sending out every day for the next thirty days, is that you immediately want to get your team to do these two things:

1.) First, get every core team member to go to the project Facebook page and ask their friends and family to "Like" it. (They'll be able to do this easily because they should all be page administrators by now.) This will immediately notify their entire friends list of the project page, which will now have your campaign video and campaign URL pinned to the top!

As soon as those page "Likes" start flooding in, the Facebook algorithms will start to kick in, in your favor, and your posts will begin to take over their newsfeeds (*muhaha!*).

2.) Second, right out of the gate, get your core team members to share the campaign pitch video to their personal Facebook page, announcing that the campaign has gone live and that they're a part of the core team! In the caption of their post, ask them to be as personal as possible and share why they're passionate about the project and helping to get it funded.

After you've done this, proceed to going over the daily to-dos which we will cover in the next section.

☐ POST AN END OF DAY UPDATE ON CAMPAIGN PAGE

At the end of launch day, make sure to post an update to the campaign page, which will automatically be sent out to all of your backers, thanking them for their support on an incredible first day. Keep it personal and show your gratitude but make it clear that there is still a long road and lots of work ahead!

Your Daily Campaign To-Do List

On the next page, you'll find your campaign manager daily to-do list! (I'll get into the details of each to-do after, but you can make copies or turn back and refer to this page at the beginning of each day.)

Your Daily Campaign To-Do List

- [ ] SEND YOUR CORE TEAM MORNING EMAIL
- [ ] CHANGE COVER PHOTO TO REFLECT DAYS LEFT
- [ ] POST 5-7 TIMES ON THE CAMPAIGN FACEBOOK PAGE
- [ ] POST 5-7 TIMES ON THE CAMPAIGN TWITTER PAGE
- [ ] SEND 30 FACEBOOK MESSAGES USING "PAD" LIST
- [ ] WRITE INDIVIDUAL THANK YOU TO EVERY BACKER
- [ ] FULFILL ALL "SOCIAL MEDIA SHOUT OUT" PERKS
- [ ] MANAGE WEEKLY EVENTS
- [ ] EXECUTE CORE TEAM ACTIONS

SENDING YOUR DAILY CORE TEAM MORNING EMAIL

Each morning, you're going to send your core team a morning email, keeping them up to speed on your progress and briefing them on the weekly events. In each of these, include their daily to-do list and send the new day's cover photo with the remaining days left as an attachment. Keep these emails optimistic and fun!

Here is the core team member daily to-do list you can share:

Core Team Daily To-Do List

- ☐ Change your cover photo to reflect days left in the campaign
- ☐ Share the pitch video to your Facebook with an update
- ☐ Post 3-5 times a day on your personal Facebook Profile
- ☐ Post 3-5 times a day on your personal Twitter profile
- ☐ Send 20 personal emails using your "PAD" list
- ☐ Send 30 Facebook Messages using your "PAD" list
- ☐ Send 20 Twitter messages
- ☐ Make 1 phone call

To hit these daily targets, core team members can use the same personal email blurb we created (Page 33) and the same Facebook message blurb we will go over on Page 52.

Also, give them the instructions we'll go over on the next page as a guideline to help them come up with things to post about to hit their 3-5 posts per platform targets.

POSTING ON FACEBOOK AND TWITTER

With your daily posts to Facebook and Twitter, there are a few important things to be mindful of.

First, make sure you include the campaign URL within the first line of every post. Something like "Another exciting day over at alaskakickstarter.com!" works. **Always include this URL in every single post you make.** I repeat: ALWAYS INCLUDE THE URL IN EVERY POST YOU MAKE! A post view is rendered useless if a viewer can't figure out how to reach the campaign page easily. Again, you want to do the work for them and make it as easy as possible for them to find it and contribute.

Next, the language you use in these posts is super important! Sometimes breaking it down by how much you need to raise per day helps. People respond to specific goal posts, so saying something like "We need to raise X amount by the end of the day to hit our goal" instead of just always referring to the total overall goal helps. Always - *no matter what* - keep the language optimistic, grateful, inclusive, and upbeat!

It can be daunting trying to come up with 5-7 original posts per day without feeling like you're repeating yourself or getting stale and driving your friends and family crazy. As a team, brainstorm some guidelines and ideas for the types of posts you can be making and always keep them fun! Here are some of the guidelines my team and I used when we were experiencing writer's block:

POSTING CATEGORIES:

Project: Story, development, behind the scenes, pictures, stills, etc.
Audience Interests: Pictures, videos, articles, similar films, shared themes, related world news
People in the project: Cast, crew, team, etc.
Weekly Event posts: Matching donors, sweepstakes, and any weekly events you're running
Specific Goals: Hit X by this time, X number of donors
Perks: Pictures or screenshots of the perks, limited edition perks when they become available
Daily Posts: Daily posts based on the day's theme
- Meme Monday / Movie Monday
- Tag Tuesday
- Women Crush Wednesday
- Throwback Thursday / Thankful Thursday
- Film Friday
- Saturday & Sunday – Whatever is trending

SENDING DAILY FACEBOOK MESSAGES

We've reached one of the most important to-do's of your entire campaign! Listen closely: **Every single day that your campaign is active, you and every member of your team must send 30 Face-**

book messages per day, working down your PAD list. (30 is the number of messages that Facebook will cap you at, per day, before it thinks you're a robot and will shut you down.)

It's absolutely imperative that you do this. Email has a 3%-7% average open rate while Facebook Messenger has a proven 98.7% open rate! Yeah ... Facebook messages work and they work *really well*. To be honest, I was a bit nervous to send these messages out to people during the first few days of my campaign but, after about a week, I was quickly seeing that the success rate from those messages was staggering! Probably 40% of old friends and contacts I messaged on Facebook ended up contributing in some way and sharing, and - not only that - were excited to do so! As for ROI for time spent, these messages were, by far, the most successful to-do for me. After seeing their success rate, I never went another day without hitting that maximum of thirty messages!

Let's be honest: it can and will feel weird and icky reaching out to some people, sometimes after years of not talking to them, just to ask for their help. But what I learned in the end was the more personal I made the messages and the more I looked at it as an opportunity to connect with old friends, the more I got over my discomfort and actually started to enjoy the process.

It'll require a bit of tact as you work your way through your "PAD" list sections but there is certainly a strategy to use for these messages. First, use language that makes them feel included in the process.

Second, by sending them to the campaign URL for the share buttons, you'll kill two birds with one stone: it asks people to share the campaign to their totally separate networks while bringing them to the campaign page where they can make their own pledge if they so choose. You can use this Facebook message blurb for these and have your core team use it as well: *(Feel free to spice up as you wish.)*

> "Hey [FIRST NAME]! As you may have seen on FB, I'm kickstarting a feature film called [PROJECT NAME] on Kickstarter. I would usually NEVER direct message somebody about something like this, but we only have __ days left until the end and need all the help we can get right now. Would you be willing to share our campaign on your Facebook and Twitter profiles? I would be deeply grateful for the help in spreading the word. I'm sorry to message you directly; [WHY THE PROJECT MEANS A LOT TO YOU *ex: "this is my first feature film and I've been working on it for the past six years to turn it into a feature this year."*] We have some incredible people on our team already and we'd love to have you join us in making this long-time dream a reality. Here's the link with all the share buttons: [YOUR CUSTOM URL]. THANK YOU so so much, [FIRST NAME]!! And don't be a stranger - let me know what's up with you!! :)
> -[YOUR NAME]"

WRITING INDIVIDUAL THANK YOUS TO EVERY BACKER

Make sure you're thanking the people who pledge to your campaign daily. Not only is it just the gracious thing to do but it helps them feel more connected to the project and more likely to help you push it. (Also keep in mind, pledges can be upped or dropped at any moment of the campaign.)

Send these thank you messages directly through Kickstarter, as soon as you can. Remember, a lot of your family and friends will be pledging for their first time and it might feel risky to input their credit card info, hit "Make Your Pledge", and send their money out into the internet ether, hoping it reaches you. These thank you notes will help them to know that their pledges were received and appreciated.

My thank you notes also included a little extra ask to encourage backers to share the project as well, pushing that campaign pitch video now pinned to the top of the Facebook page.

Here's the exact note I sent out. Feel free to use it for yourself:

Racheal Cain Stephens
September 12, 2018

Thank you so much for your pledge, Jeff!!! Your support really means the world to me. I am so pumped to get this movie made and I couldn't do it without you!

You have done so much already, but if you're feelin extra supportive, feel free to help us get the word out! Share our Kickstarter video, add http://alaskakickstarter.com/ to a post, or chat up a neighbor- all of it truly adds up.

Thank you!! x
Racheal

Week Two

*A huge CONGRATS on making it through your week one!
You should be proud of yourself.*

Your second week should run similarly to your first. You'll follow your daily to-do checklist and have your core team continue to do the same. The pledges coming in will start to slow drastically this week but don't fret! This is normal. Just keep a steady pace and do these extra few things this week:

☐ POST ANOTHER UPDATE TO THE CAMPAIGN PAGE

Utilize the power of campaign updates to reach all of your backers at once. (Once you post an update, it'll automatically send an email to all of your backers with it.) Thank them for an incredible first week, inform them of your goals for the upcoming week ("We want to hit 50% by Friday", etc.), and let them know that, now that you're past the first week, you're going to need their help more than ever in spreading the word. Request that they share your campaign video to their personal Facebook pages and spread the word to anyone who might be interested in hearing about and supporting the project.

☐ POST A VIDEO UPDATE TO YOUR FACEBOOK PAGE

Post a video update to your Facebook page and personal profile, and encourage your core team to do the same. Don't worry about making this video look professional (I used my iPhone and was sometimes still in my pajamas) - just keep it personal. Photos are great but there's nothing like a video to reach people directly. Also, Facebook algorithms favor video content and will organically push them for you. Share about your progress, your goals for the upcoming week, and any upcoming events you have planned.

☐ POST IN FACEBOOK GROUPS WITH SIMILAR AUDIENCES

While pledges from your friends and family will start to slow this week (as those who are going to donate likely already have), it's time to start doing some additional outreach of your own.

Remember those Facebook groups you joined the week before launch? Go back into them and share a post in each, telling members about your project, why you're passionate about it, and why you think they'd be interested. Use photos or videos, if you can, for added attention.

Note: I didn't have an enormous amount of success here, probably since my project was more emotion-driven and I was a stranger to these people, but I thought it was worth mentioning because other campaigns, such as those for cool and useful products, might see better results. I did get a couple click-throughs and pledges though - better than nothing!

☐ CREATE A FACEBOOK EVENT FOR YOUR HALFWAY POINT

Again, utilize the power of Facebook events and create a Facebook event for your campaign's halfway mark. Set the date to the 15th day of your campaign and the time to 1pm. Invite a different set of 500 people from your Facebook friends list, specifically people who haven't donated to the campaign thus far. (Your master "PAD" list will come in handy again here to make sure you're hitting up different people every time.)

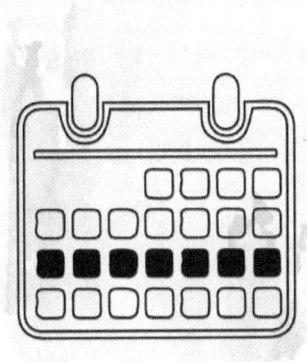

Week Three

More than halfway there! ... It'll all be worth it in just two short weeks.

Pledges will start to slow even more this week but hang tight and stick to your to-do lists! It's a marathon and, while I know you're exhausted by this point, just keep a steady pace. Follow through with your daily to-do lists and keep your team's moral high! Post another update to your campaign page to welcome new backers, post another personal video update to Facebook, run your weekly event, post in more Facebook groups with similar audiences and, finally, create another Facebook event; this time for your campaign's final 48 hours. Have your core team help you to invite the maximum of 500 people from your "PAD" lists who haven't yet donated.

Note: It can be truly nerve-wrecking as pledges can seem to slow to a halt throughout this week. I just want to reassure you that this is completely normal! It's called your "campaign plateau". Everyone I've spoken with remembers going through it and how frightening it was when they were yet to meet their goals. Stay positive, conserve energy, and rest assured that your final week is going to be a BIG one!

The Final Week

The homestretch. Give yourself a pat on the back, then do some stretches because this final week will be BIG.

In the final week of your campaign, refer to your "PAD" list and make note of anyone in your "Personal" section, or anyone you had considered "highly likely to donate" who hasn't yet pledged.

Throughout the week, email or Facebook message these people with one last subtle nudge to donate. I've learned that people are surprisingly great procrastinators. Assume the best and say something like *"I just wanted to reach out one last time, so you don't miss the opportunity to be a part of it"* etc. Always pitch it as an opportunity to be included and remind them that the clock is almost up!

Once you've revisited your "PAD" list and reached out to anyone who hasn't donated, carry on with your regular campaign weekly to-dos, including that final big weekly event. Post one last campaign update, 48 hours before the clock is up, and ask all of your backers to give the campaign one final "share". Treat them like team members now.

You should see a surge in pledges in your final 72 hours, especially right before your campaign hits fully funded. Nevertheless, follow through with thanking every new backer, all the way up until your final day. Then, feel free to collapse into a very long and well-deserved post-campaign nap.

You freaking DID IT. I'm so proud.

When To Rest

Throughout the craziness of campaigning and the few months beforehand, there was so much work to do at every moment of the day. I quite literally spent every waking hour behind my computer for the four weeks we were live and, with so much to tend to, I never knew when the right time was to just *rest*. There was one stretch where I eventually realized I hadn't slept in two and a half days and I was nearing a complete burnout. My brain felt like it had fried into scrambled eggs and I could barely keep my burning, computer-screen-seared eyes open.

You have to know when to rest and, when that time comes - *do it*. Force yourself to unplug, turn off, and recharge ... or else you will eventually reach a breaking point. Getting the proper amount of sleep each night will lead to higher efficiency anyway.

Know when to rest. Sleep during the Midnight-8am window in the time zone where the majority of your audience lives. You can find this exact information on your Facebook Page under "Insights" -> "People" and also in the "Insights" tab of your (now business) Instagram page.

This may seem obvious but, sometimes your primary audience is based in a different time zone. Personally, I crowdfunded in south Florida while 80% of my audience on social media was based in Los Angeles. For this reason, I did my best to sleep from midnight-8am PST, even though that meant waking at 11am EST and going to sleep at 3am EST. It felt strange to get such a late start in the day, but it turned out to be most effective to rest up when the majority of my audience was sleeping.

Also, use weekends and that middle ground "campaign plateau" to rest and recover. Things will go quieter during these periods anyway, so use them to recharge. Social media activity drops drastically over the weekends, which means don't be afraid to let up a bit and unplug. Posts you might be making during this time wouldn't be seen as much anyway. Get out and get some sunshine! See a friend for coffee. Give yourself a well-deserved (though inevitably short) break wherever possible. It's important to be at the top of your game Monday-Friday, so plan accordingly!

Final Thoughts

Before I sign off and send you on your way to go off and run your big, successful crowdfunding campaign, I wanted to leave you with some final thoughts.

FOCUS ON FACEBOOK AS YOUR MAIN PLATFORM

First - I'll say it one last time - focus on Facebook as your main platform in the months before you campaign and while crowdfunding. Instagram has been wonderful for me with how visual and straightforward it is, but I noticed almost immediately during this campaign that most of my Kickstarter traffic was coming directly from my Facebook Page (where I had a much smaller audience)! I never really focused my energy on growing the Facebook because I think it always seemed a bit more complicated to me and, honestly, I didn't love the idea of intermixing the project with my personal family and friends posts, because it felt somewhat spammy. But there's always a way of doing so authentically.

Learn from my mistake! While growing a social following and then ultimately crowdfunding, I'd highly advise steering your efforts toward building up your project's Facebook more than any other platform. In the end, Facebook came through with about 33% of pledges, all coming through direct traffic, vs about 25% of the pledges through "Kickstarter advanced discovery" and our project getting onto the main "Project We Love" page. About 12% were direct through our Instagram. And the rest was pretty evenly split between Twitter/Reddit/Google/other little Kickstarter sections.

Of course, you're going to reap rewards wherever you put in the effort but I was surprised to learn Facebook was such a dominating source of pledges. The site offers fantastic analytics and incomparable advertising tools, allowing you to connect with very specific audiences. At the end of the day, they offer a reach that no other platform can contend with - so do what I would, if I were starting from scratch, and spend your time and energy there!

MY BIGGEST MISTAKES

While we're on the topic of things I'd do differently, I wanted to share my biggest mistakes with you to save you from making them. We've covered them briefly throughout but let's recap:

I felt my biggest mistake of all was not doing enough preparation in building out my core team. I think I looked at it more like "who can I get to help me do this?" rather than "who would be the best campaigners to bring on?". Again, look for friends with the biggest voices on social media and look for people you don't share many friends with, so your core team has further reach. I brought on a lot of family and friends with overlapping networks and, ultimately, there was a lot of crossover and wasted advertising efforts. It's a lot of work but, with the right incentives, you can orchestrate some great help and grow a strong team that will get you to your big goal in no time!

My next biggest mistake had me kicking myself for weeks afterward: It was simply not sending those 30 Facebook messages per day in the beginning. It was priceless time I knew I could never get back. At the end of my 30 day campaign, there were still probably 100 people on my "PAD" list who I hadn't had the chance to message. I couldn't help but wonder how many more pledges I could've garnered from those, had I used those incredibly effective Facebook DMs. You live and you learn, right? Learn from my mistake and send your maximum of thirty every day.

Finally, another mistake I definitely made was not having a clear sharable timeline to share with my team. This was the result of simply running out of time in my preparation. I actually didn't know what my fourth weekly event would be until week three, and was scrambling to come up with something. This required so much extra energy and effort and, again, ate up that valuable time while your campaign is live that you can't get back.

Prepare, prepare, and prepare some more and you will undoubtedly reach your big goal!

DON'T UNDERESTIMATE HOW MUCH PEOPLE WILL WANT TO HELP YOU

This could go easily under the My Biggest Mistakes section too, but it's so crucial that I wanted to leave it as my final note to you. One thing I had to overcome really early on (and maybe this was more of a personal hurdle, but I'm sure some of you will relate) was how uncomfortable I felt reaching out and asking for help. It took me a few days to wiggle my way out of my shell and stand tall in the spotlight. But you've got to put yourself out there for what you love and, in the end, people will respect you for it.

In the beginning, I was timid with my asks. But, by the end, I realized that the beauty of crowdfunding is in welcoming others to be a part of your journey - inviting them in and including them in what matters to you. And I was so surprised to find how many people were excited to be welcomed in like that.

I totally underestimated how much people would want to help and genuinely be excited to be a part of my project. Don't underestimate anyone. Don't sell yourself short.

It is perhaps the thing that makes us most human - our need for connection and our need to be needed. Allow others to help you! Invite them in. Open the doors and windows to this project that means so much to you. You'll be surprised by the ripple effects of doing so and the people you'll inspire in the process.

I know you're an independent person who makes things happen for yourself - that is already clear - but, take it from me .... you cannot and will never be able to go it entirely alone. We all need each other and that is, perhaps, what I learned most while crowdfunding. I can honestly say that, through the struggle, sweat, and (many many) tears of it all, crowdfunding cracked me open and made me a better person. I'm so excited for you to begin your journey, push yourself to places you didn't know were possible, and have your own epic experience you'll remember for the rest of your days. I truly hope this guide helps you to see how possible it all really is.

Now go out and raise the funds to make your wildest dream your reality! ... You're as ready as you'll ever be.

-Racheal

www.ingramcontent.com/pod-product-compliance
Lightning Source LLC
Chambersburg PA
CBHW030730180526
45157CB00008BA/3122